T0161200

THE

THEORY

OF THE

LOSER CLASS

THE

THEORY

OF THE

LOSER CLASS

JON PAUL FIORENTINO

———

A WORK IN THREE PARTS.

COACH HOUSE BOOKS

MMVI.

Canada Council   Conseil des Arts
for the Arts   du Canada

 ONTARIO ARTS COUNCIL
CONSEIL DES ARTS DE L'ONTARIO

Canadä

Published with the assistance of the Canada Council for the Arts and
the Ontario Arts Council. We also acknowledge the financial support
of the Government of Canada through the Book Publishing Industry
Development Program (BPDIP).

LIBRARY AND ARCHIVES CANADA CATALOGUING IN PUBLICATION

Fiorentino, Jon Paul
    The theory of the loser class / Jon Paul Fiorentino.

Poems.
ISBN 1-55245-168-2

    I. Title.

PS8561.I585T44 2006   C811'.6   C2C006-901138-9

for Tara and Lilly

Veblen's evil eye is fertile
— Theodor Adorno

loss leaders

I'm not suggesting we're all losers
I'm insisting upon it

LOSS LEADERS

A retail conceit:

Veblen in the liquidation bin
buried under chromium dioxide tapes

Canonicity stacked against
the revolving door

A young man acicular
A latent coercivity

RAPIDCYCLER

We don't have much time left
so please don't touch me

~

It's just because I'm saccharine
and sacred

~

If I could change anything about us
it would be our area code

~

The slowest rapidcycler in the wide world —
unhook me from the drip

~

We are all entitled to our own hyperbole
especially you

~

Montreal has made a fool of me
for the second-last time

THERMOSTRAT

The edit will leave you
empty

Iron censure
re: formatted now

c:/ drive
straight through the living room

busted
frigid
aire

wish I brought my template
to keep me warm

MEMORY CARD

This poem finds you convincing the screensaver to make countless appearances; you monitor your calls, save your dreams on a memory card. Pine for scripts that call for your flair for the Latinate rewrite, your talent for heart-wrenching pratfalls. You're missing the application. // And you can't quite explain it – you don't notice the rain anymore; you walk for hours between old Wolseley houses and invoke the names of retired NDP MLAS, a movement toward the great abstractions. // You want none of it; it's all yours. You feel hemmed in; show it well with the precious few linguistic tricks you still remember. Remember: there is always another shift, always another song until the last one. // There are always fewer suitable days, more people, more opportunities, fewer chances. Turn off the soundtrack. It's digital. There is no desire left in you. For slip-page, to break your neck on the shag carpet again and again. And this poem finds you. Stored in an antique memory card. Looking for the cheat codes.

SO MENTAL

Fluoxetine mends the comforter
of the mind only
so mental

Imipramine
glorious late last night
so cerebral

Amwegian salespersons sold me
some soap
so bathe me

Safewegian security chased me
good as busted
so jail me

Snobbery schlocked me
felt logical
so sinful

240-VOLT NATIONAL CONSERVATORY
(after Grandaddy)

Air-conditioner anxiety: flop sweat synchrony, apocrine odour sheathes the 240-Volt National Conservatory. // Repairmen and -women strap themselves to dishwasher doors, capillary tubes on their sleeves. Cylindrical cicadas gurgle and creak universal nostalgia – without fail in the land of failure. Misused fuses line the countryside, up to and away from the 240-VNC. // Machines petrified by the thought of leaving, fears amplified under the grid, inconceivable power outside. And the conservationists: fossils with power washers. The air drenched with the promise of liquid courage.

RIGHT IN THE SPINE

Crooning Gertrude Stein's songs
but sounding shallow, somehow

Arrived in style but
can't get off your bike

Time to slash prices
on the Paxil and shovels

I've listened intently (almost)
to the revisionist chorus:

If a loser falls
I feel it

And if a loser falls
I feel it

INCURSION

Radio will never. The absurd beautiful broadcast words. Last.

A stone's throw from my cell
construction has already begun.

I heard incorrectly. My reception is terrible and I'm feeling
                                                    settled.

I've a kick-ass TV. No insurance. No words except 'incursion.'
I like it. I want to sell it.

CONTRIBUTRONS

like lice

settle lattice

epiphanies pipedreams

roles loser

stale elastic

pedant mental

hole

THE INTERNET BROKEN

The internet broken
the radio dead air
the TV snow
the poet boring

The snow radio
the TV air
the boring internet
the dead broken poet

EPIPHIST

There's more than one way to mind a store
don't forget to water the cash registers

Loss leaders sprawl on the bathroom floor
funny now but

My persecution complex is emblematic
say it with a used Telecaster

Find ways out
epiphanic

Clean. Jerk.

BACKWARD

Don't call me anymore
play the video game backward

Don't give away the ending
play the telephone home

Don't make me finish
play the Chevette northward

Don't bother to signal
play the text inward

Don't listen to the pedagogue
play it

JUMPDRIVE HERPES

Sparring spores
compound stunners

A two-four of
isopropyl alcohol coolers

The skin
for basement clubbing

Lost elastic
home hub comfort

Zip disks call
their patronizing agents

Robots play, get
JumpDrive herpes

Software leaks all
over, all over

STET

Stuck to the joystick
tethered to the console
joined to the socket
linked to the transformer
tied to the substation
sucking on the grid

FRONT-FACED

10 want as in
20 lack as in
30 went as in
40 lent as in
50 wuss as in
60 loss as in
70 wash as in
80 lush as in
90 goto 10

DELVER

You can't spread against a bet
sprawl out now

You can't bring an intravenous to work
work at womb

You can't help but delve without a spine
or can you

You can't Photoshop yourself a life
deploy stupid verb

SONNET OF R2-D2

Tweet blip blip doot tweet blip blip doot beewoo
Deep vreee wop vreet; vree waap deep beep vreet woo
Twooo beep dee vroop dee vroot vroop vreep burrwaap
Doop deep beewoo burrwaap vreet dooop – beewoo!
Beewoo whoot wop eeeet oooo burrwaap burrwaap.
Bwop bwoop blip breeet bip bop beep breeoo, breeoo
breeoo blip doot. Vreet tweet burr waap deep doop
burr waap breeeet vroot vroot beewoo beep braap woo.
Vreet deep! Vreet deep! Vroot bap beewoo breeoo!
Oooo breeet deep. Oooo breeet deep. Beewoo bip bip.
Vroot bap! Vroot beep! Vreet beewoo bap breeoo!
Oooo bip whoot vroot whoot dee tweet waap bip bip.

Whoot whirr eeeet bip tweet blip woo beep breeoo?
Wop woo vreet oooo vroot beewoo braap burrwaap!

BINARY CODE SONNET 1.0

```
01001001001000000011000110110000101101110100100100
01110100001000000011000100110010101011011000110100 1
01100101011101100110010100100000011110010110111 1
01110101001000000011000100110111101111011010001101000
01100101011100100110010101001000010000001110100
01101111001000000111010001110010011000010110111 0
01110011011011000110000101111010001100101010000110 1
00001010011101000110100001101001011100110010000 0
01110011011011110110111100110111001100101011101 00
00100000011011010110000101100100011001010010010 0 0 0 0
0110111101100110001000000100110001100011000010111010 0
01101001011011100110000101110100011001010010010 0 0 0 0
01110011011111001011011100111010001100001011110 00
00101100000011010000010100111010001101010000110100 1
0111001100100000011001100110000101101001010110110 0
0111010101110010011001010010000001101111011011001 10
00100000011000010010000001110110011001010101110010
01110011011010010110011001101001011100011011000001
01110100011010010101101111011011100010111000001101
00001010010010010010000000110001101110000101101110
10010010011101000001000000110001001100101011011000
01101001011001010111011001100101001000000011110 0 1
01101111011101010010000001100110111010001101111
011011000110010100100000011010001101000011010001
011100110010000001100110011110101011000110110101 1
01101001011011100110011100100000011000100110111 1
0110111101101011001011100000110100001010010010010 0 1
0111010010010010011100110010000001100010010011011 1
01110010011010010110111100110011100100000011000 0 1
01101111001100100000010000001101001011101001001001 0
01110011001000000111001101111010101011000110110100 0
001000000011000010010000001101111011010000010111001 1
01110100011001010010000001101111011001100001000000
01110100011010010110110101011001010010010111000001101
```

000010100000110100001010010101000110100001100101
001000000110001001101111011100100110010101100100
011011110110110100100000011011110110011000100000
011101000110100001100101001000000110100101100001
011011010110001000100000011010010111001100100000
011010010111010001100110010000001101111011101111
011011100001101000010100111001101101011110110111 0
011001110010000001100001011011100110010000100000
011101000110111100100000011101000110100001100100 1
011100110010000001100110110111101101011100110011 1
001000000111011101100101001000000110100001100001
011101100110010010010000000110001001100101011 00101
011011100010000011101000111001001110101011 00101
001011100001101000010100100000100100000001101100
011000010110001001101111011101101010101 11001100101
011001000010000001110010011010000111100101110100
011010000110110100100000011000010110111001100100
001000000110000100100000011101000111010101101110
011001010110110001100101011100110110110011001 00000
011100110110001101101011110111001001100101100101 11
000011010000010100101000001100101011101000111001 0
011000010111001001100011011010000110000101101110
001000000110010001110010011011110110111001100101
001011000010000001110011011111001011100000110 1000
011010010110110001101001011101000110100101100011
001000000110010001101001011100110110110000011000 01
011101000110001101101000000101100000011010000101 0
011100110110110000101100100000100000011100110110 0101
011101000110110001101001011100110111010000010 0000
011011110110111000010000000111010001101010001100101
001000000110011001101100011011110110111101110010
001000000110001001100101011001100110110111101110010
011001010010000001110100011010000110010100100000
011100110110100001101111111011101110010110000001101

000010100111010101110000011101110110000101110010
011001000110110001111001001000000110110101101111
011000100110100101101100011001010010000001100111
011001010110111001110010010010010000000101110100
011001010111010001101000011001010111001001100101
011001000010000001100100011011110111011011011101110
001011000000110100000101001110000011100100110 1001
011011010010000001100001011011100110010000010 0000
011100000111001001100101011100110111011101000 01101001
011011100110010010000001101100011010010111000 00
001000000111001101100101011100100111011011000 10000100000
011000110110010100101100001000000110001101101111
011011010110011001101111011100100111010000000 1100011011011 01111
011011010110011001101111011100100111010000000 1100011011011 01111
011011010110111011001100110111110111001001110 10000100000
011010000111100101011011010101101011100010111 000001101
000010100000110100000101001010101000110100001 100101
011100100110010100100000011000010111001001100 100110010 1
001000000110110101100001010110111100111100100 100100000
011100010111010101100101011100110110111101000 1101001
011011110110111011001110010010000001101111011 00110 0
001000000111010001101000011010000100001011001 100100000
011100110110000101011001000010000001100110011 01101111
011100100110100101101001000000000110100001010 01000010
011101010111010000010000000111010001101010000 1100101
001000000110111101101101110011011000111100100 100100000
011000010110111001110011011011011101101001010 1110010
001000000111010001101000011010000110000101110 10000100000
011101101101101111011100100110101101011011001 100100000
011010010101110011001000000100100110111101000 1110111
011011110010111010010101000000110100001010

I can't believe you bothered to translate
this sonnet made of Latinate syntax,
this failure of a versification.
I can't believe you stole this fucking book.
It's boring and it's such a waste of time.

The boredom of the iamb is its own
song and so to this song we have been true.
A laboured rhythm and a tuneless score —
Petrarchan drone, syphilitic dispatch,
sad set list on the floor before the show,
upwardly mobile genre tethered down,
prim and pristine lip service, comfort hymn.

There are many questions of this sad form
But the only answer that works is 'two.'

JOYSTICKS

Here is a plane
of thrumming joysticks

Press here land
scrape

TV SONG

Exorcist loser
nurtured life

                    Projective loser
                    typo, negative

Die loser
frustrate cast rate

                    Noose loser
                    loosen ink

Grip loser
knit to knot

                    Toxic loser
                    trick glass

Pedagogic loser
slip sicken

                    Secret loser
                    slap happy

Vex loser
ex oh

                    Plummet loser
                    crypt quicken

Vorpal loser
shunned snatch

                    Spawn loser
                    convention then

Negative loser
tertiary faced

                    Want loser
                    cheque mate

THE ERRAND BOY

You almost drown
penmanship fade

Idiot dive stooge
everybody loves a rat

Pull off the short
sight gag

Your talent keeps you
warm at nap time

You deliver the mail
you phone it in (you delver)

Everyone uses you
to need you

Puppets can't talk
but you're a good listener

We are all errand boys
all Morty S. Tashmans

Except you, for some
reason

You are Jerry Lewis

JERRY LEWIS AND A GUN
(NYC 2005)

Slip nostalgic, name-drop Al Jolson
clench your teeth for the callback

You're a luxury sedan, late-night Broadway
I'm an electrode in your spine

A grand piano hardly played
you're a molested Hammond

You engage in regretful punchline
diction, flop sweat flatline, starlet fever

Endless pratfall theory
gestures beyond the host

Bad aim. Exquisite timing.

January 18, 2005

Two days to go. I went past the Ed Sullivan Theater today and, as the crowd filtered out, I slipped in. I saw Paul and the band but no Dave. Security spotted me crouched behind a chair in the second-last row.

Solvent,
Jonny

Whip out your pain vibrator
and howl an endorsement

Twitch a self-portrait
dust on the screen

Dirge flicker
the cathode ray will fade

Forget the LCD
your pixels are brittle

You're a vector
I have a gun

But I'm at home
and you're not there yet

January 19, 2005

Spent the day at home. Looking over poems. I think I have been infelicitous. I normally don't talk like this. Why would I write like this? I tend toward pre-emptive elegy. I mean to tell you what this entry consists of, then I will write the entry, then I will tell you it has been written. I forget practice in favour of theory. This is unreadable. And the poem? Tomorrow it's just me, Jerry Lewis and a gun.

Errant boy,
Jonny

This is the way my show goes:

I settle in the studio audience, back row
gonna shoot you like it's 1946

Halfway through the first segment
I shoot you with my thin revolver

Letterman hands you a towel
to soak up the blood

Commercial break   we're back
now you're behind the desk

Paul Shaffer revives you
with a prop defibrillator

Wearing blood-stained fake teeth
I'm in the guest chair

Time to say goodnight

January 20, 2005

I don't like ending on a snivel, but it was all I could muster. Mastery of form is beyond me. I'm drenched tonight, never made it inside the theatre. Ever called out your name by mistake? I have. How chronic is that? So insensitive, such a loser.

Lost,
Jonny

selected lies

We are all in the gutter
but some of us are looking at the scars

SELECTED LIES

I can't name names

I drop them

this will be a long poem

about home

tell your MLA

or

tell your MNA

but

tell it scant

BORING PEOPLE HOLDING HANDS

Let's break into every Sunday School supply room, take all the construction paper, safety scissors and glue sticks and make the largest chain of paper dolls this city's ever seen. // We'll call it 'Boring People Holding Hands' and we'll wrap it around the financial district. It will make us feel better and get us out of the house. // Maybe the paper-doll chain will succumb to weather or public taste. Maybe it will teach everyone a lesson of some sort. // Maybe careerist couples will hold hands and skip through puddles and maybe giddy blurbists will make their own chains and maybe morose merchandisers will give in to their hunger and choke on non-toxic red crayons.

LOSER DOWN

on St. Marc Street

ready for the body bag

unforgiving railing
dramatic gestures
best performed indoors

angelic paramedics
a stretcherful
of ambivalence

DRENCH

Drenched whiskey jack
limp limbic iamb

Scrape fence climb
snap-button shirt

Payphone prayer drift
tonic tact breach

Primp proper prick
heart-wrenching John

Take the 14 bus
get off, drench yourself

GRAHAM MALL SUITE

Abandoned walkers glimmer, mad trams trembling
all day where shoppers won't tread

Windows beckon soot
the doorways settle
for

If I had the means, oxygen would burn through these grey
expanses
bloated babies would beguile from storefronts

The mayor would breakdance daily at noon

I have a loudspeaker and some free time
I have a mind to not stray

Come down

I will make the posters
you buy the paste

On second thought, don't leave home
just throw me a phone call and we'll meet between another
nowhere

Graham Mall, Winnipeg planners say,
is a major vein

Oxygen blanket
funereal flats

Everyone comes
on their way to elsewhere

Funeral home
insurance blaze

The city in its hospital gown
transit abrasive blanket fare

Tram recursion every hour
the infinite sentence living here

Ironic dative resident shift:
Graham Mall mythology

I can't begin to tell you how I got here
I can't begin to tell you how I got her

Like home
for the shifted and non

Disavow the term 'bus' —
indefinite incursion by no one in particular

The trams miss their cables
varicose line in a sullen centre

Endless religion
and arson enthusiasts

VIA GRAHAM MALL
(song for Earle Nelson)

I am with you tonight, Earle Nelson, as I drag my rope
through the snow from Smith to Vaughan

A memory lapse. I have thought
of changing my name

The rooms are harder to rent by the day
squalor as potential

St. Boniface calling or taunting
Headingley an alternate case

My victims: IT workers, lounge singers, dental assistants
my methods: charming anachronistic; my mood: subjunctive

If only
the constables were literate

Strangulation dates itself
I will wear a whipcord suit and a pocket watch

For now, I sulk through the great unplowed
the city an unwashed comforter

Mrs. Emily Patterson in the arsoned ashes
splinter and wreckage of Broadway

You are with me tonight
Earle Nelson

The potential of a ten-foot extension cord
the limitations of sainthood

EARLE NELSON PRESENTS
FUN WITH SUFFIXATION

Affixatory
Bruticity
Constability
Dirgesque
Earleless
Frostant
Ghostic
Hangnailed
Intertextured
Jailiation
Killthrift
Lifed
Misanthropian
Noosened
Oxygenism
Pattersonessence
Quixoticity
Rationaleness
Suffocational
Thorsteiny
Unrepentantonic
Veblenier
Winnipeggiest
Xenophobical
Yelloween
Zealoticiousness

EARLE NELSON HOUSE

Nelson refused to bathe
romance, to waver

Nomadic dementia:
Minneapolis drove a dark star north

Quiet and the restless afternoon
Salvarsan anti-syphilis raid

All quiet at the boarding house
switch off the evening

Personation:
love results in its own undoing, or whatever

The constable's revolver drawn at dawn, or whenever
gallows used sometime after

Earle Nelson's cervical dislocation
slow, bathed in recognition

THE GHOSTS OF ELIM CHAPEL

There are no ghosts
who particularly despise the building

Destroyed in 1974
rebuilt as a spectre, fictional

It occurs to me that I tipped the first candle
roughly the same time I was born

I openly admit culpability
as we all should, culpable or not

Reticent children
leaving the sermon, trudging to Sunday school

Trapped

It went down like this:
the flames rose, the air departed

FOREIGN WEED

A trail of loosestrife led me
home

Always maintained a semblance of balance
the challenge to temporality

That is to say
I'm lonely or lonesome or both

At least
it was a nice ride

An easy challenge
an impossible morning

Don't forget to miss the
longest losing streak ever

Impossible to miss me
not winning

STRAFED

Rows of snowplows
grafted over a defective street

Mentoring scribes toward whiplash
defected, defeatist

Cocaine beams
through a theory lens

Menthol mentor
tricyclic

Strafed on
a futon

Cognition goes on
without us

THE THEORY OF THE LOSER CLASS

Alpha male
        Aleph naught

Let this be agented expeditiously
however drudged or relatively unfit
we may be for social commerce

We have, by tacit means, an imperative
to press on, and strength in numbers

If we must be subservient, submissive
then let us be this way in accordance
with this text, industrious as it may appear

There will be no more barbarism
welcome to the 'we deserve' era

Let us serve ourselves
exploit ourselves

We are the motherfucking chess club[1]

1   *Industry is effort that goes to create a new thing, with a new purpose given it by the fashioning hand of its maker out of passive ('brute') material; while exploit, so far as it results in an outcome useful to the agent, is the conversion to his own ends of energies previously directed to some other end by an other agent.*

—Veblen

Thorstein was the
captain of the chess club

Until his unfortunate
anachronism

At the window
wanting

Neighbourhood kids thrive
tactless

How can we compare
conspire

Parents drive in and out of ownership
inattentive

The decade dissolves
we sprawl

Run over
still[2]

2   *An invidious comparison is a process of valuation of persons in respect of worth.*

— Veblen

We built a fort
in the basement

Out of cardboard boxes
and knitted blankets

Turned out the lights
took off our clothes

Thorstein got super scared
fled in his gitch

PREMATURE DEVOUT OBSERVANCES

Leader
Scam

Leisure
Swine

Lesson
Seam

Labour
Sour

Lesion
Serve

Tryst
Cyst[3]

3   *The normal and characteristic occupations of the class in this mature phase of its life history are in form very much the same as in its earlier days. These occupations are government, war, sports, and devout observances.*
—Veblen

We colonized Thorstein's backyard
in the name of suburban sprawl

Replaced his childhood
with linguistic pathologies

It was a gentle birth
(however drunk the doctor was reported to be)

(however ambivalent Mother)
(however absent Father)

I reportedly managed my way through the fray
antedating myself with historic flair

Glimpsing the good doctor's premeditated
intent, breached, honorific smirk concealed

The ceremonial differentiation of the dietary
pecuniary strength incipient

Welcome to St. Boniface Hospital
(this calls for a drunk)

Welcome to the miserable,
the predatory, TV[4]

---

4   *Drunkenness and the other pathological consequences of the free use
of stimulants therefore tend in their turn to become honorific, as being a
mark, at the second remove, of the superior status of those who are able to
afford the indulgence.*

—Veblen

The moment Thorstein
saw the good doctor

He became suspicious of
partum and post-partum methodologies

After syntax
the fringes are where it's at

Festive retrogression
polyester centrifuge

Centripetal pedalling
beaming antonyms

Radiant
bodies

Literary
deflowery

The cent where it wasn't never
the sentences, whatever[5]

<hr />

5   *It takes time for any change to permeate the mass and change the*
habitual attitude of the people; and especially it takes time to change the
habits of those classes that are socially more remote from the radiant body.
                                                                      −Veblen

Thorstein, to be deflowered
in the church basement

Had trouble
shedding his britches

Cut and paste dactylic reason
squalor, splendour, trochaic flailings

Reward yourself with tenet etchings
cynical cipher conventions, clinical

Then take the piss with von Humboldt,
finite use of finite means, an endless countability

All of this for not meeting the requirements
of some discernment, for not getting laid

Exert shun tactics, dark leisure, snob method,
and, in doing so, kill linguistic bugs dead[6]

6   *Under the selective surveillance of the law of conspicuous waste there grows up a code of accredited canons of consumption, the effect of which is to hold the consumer up to a standard of expensiveness and wastefulness in his consumption of goods and in his employment of time and effort.*
—Veblen

Thorstein revisited his youth under the surveillance
of scrupulous cultural critics

He chose to act formally
more or less

Safety
tense

Crimped
eyeliner

Density
tease

Gravity
sag

Acrid
wash

Maiden
Transcona[7]

7   Our dress, therefore, in order to serve its purpose effectually, should not only be expensive, but it should also make plain to all observers that the wearer is not engaged in any kind of productive labor.

                                                            — *Veblen*

Thorstein fired from various jobs
for failing to adhere

Finally found a home
loss-prevention officer at Sears

Then
well

It's blonde everywhere tonight
well-crafted

Soothed on the jar outside of womb
so glad he has this problem

Knows so very few verbs that
work for culture

Drunken doctors
drift through life in outlying elements

(Just one last thrust
and TV gets the hell outta Dodge)

He spent all his patience inside the womb
melancholic canon geography

Now counting his days in
uncountable nouns and it doesn't really[8]

---

8   *The man of our industrial communities tends to breed true to one or the other of three main ethnic types; the dolichocephalic-blond, the brachycephalic-brunette, and the Mediterranean — disregarding minor and outlying elements of our culture.*

— Veblen

Thorstein was born
with jet-black hair

Thirty years later
late fees ensued

Reversion works this way:

a stubborn oeuvre
subsistence, only form

We deserve
get ready

Variation works this way:

Scoff but it will only swell
your well-intentioned couplet

Neighbourhood kids
get theirs

Industry works this way:

Shock treatment
detriment

I'm late
I'm late[9]

---

9   *The man of the hereditary present is slightly archaic as judged for the*
purposes of the latest exigencies of associated life. And the type to which the
modern man chiefly tends to revert under the law of variation is a some-
what more archaic human nature.

—Veblen

Thorstein's sitcom
was cancelled

Miscast, he crawled back to
public access

Government, war, spurts, and
devout observances:

Every day is Labour Day
every day is insolent

Excess theory bedhead
emulation sham brigade

Effort in the sewing circle
emergency boy's room tavern

Elemental schisms aggregate
engaging valuations congregate

Erasing variant
ethic typography

End-game surveillance
end-game sanctioned[10]

---

10 *So there are 'boys' brigades,' and other organizations, under clerical*
sanction, acting to develop the emulative proclivity and the sense of status
in the youthful members of the congregation.

—Veblen

One night, Thorstein broke into the high school
slipped into the Home Economics lab

Sewed circles around himself
until he could glimpse the perfect reversion[11]

11 *No theory here.*

Survival of a Non-Invidious Interest

Then Thorstein lost it[12]

---

12 *There, there.*

THEODORIAN IN GRAY

adorned
features
hypostatic
progress inbuilt
cultural short shrift
just capitalist period
means nothing
just flow
just fad
just

vitriolic
lineation iced
mere immediacy
progress saccharine preen
supremacy technocratic
barbaric doctrine
replay tilt
until

world
walking stick
trite supremacy
cultural flameout
(just take that)
a just meant
causality
bites art
state a
greed

takes
obsolete
form ation
non sense no seqs
sport religion
decor egress
culture
blame
blam

insignia
nation nostalgic
spleen dual shtick
industry kitsch
lust shot
practice
makes
prefect

SPINE

Purchase the derelict bundle
upgrade now to
Swindle v2.0

Use prescriptive usage
ply the canon of honorific waste
a predatory occupation

The meddle class
piratic and elemental
siphon verse solvents

Abject voyeur drones
common run of men
these aren't the druids you're looking for